"To Baby Olivia, Mommy &
Daddy -
Enjoy these "Little" books
with "Big" wisdom in them
as you share special times
together!

Love,
Carl, Vicky, Aaron & Jared
Burke

MW01200046

2006

Written and compiled by Lois Rock
Illustrations copyright © 2003 by Katherine Lucas
Text copyright © 2003 by Lion Publishing
First published in Great Britain in 2003 by Lion
Publishing.

First U.S. Edition

LCCN: 2003108019

10 9 8 7 6 5 4 3 2 1

Acknowledgments

The extracts in this book have been inspired by or
adapted from the biblical verses noted in each case,
unless otherwise stated. Second Bible extract on p. 6
quoted from the Good News Bible, published by The
Bible Societies/HarperCollins Publishers Ltd, UK ©
American Bible Society 1996, 1971, 1976, 1992, used
with permission.

Printed in Singapore

The illustrations for this book were done in acrylic on
textured acrylic paper.

The text was set in Garamond BE.

Little Words of Wisdom

FROM THE BIBLE

Lois Rock

Illustrated by Katherine Lucas

LITTLE, BROWN AND COMPANY

New York ⌁ An AOL Time Warner Company

Above All

Love God with all your heart.
Love God with all your soul.
Love God with all your strength.

from Deuteronomy 6:5

Love your neighbor as you love
yourself.

Leviticus 19:18

Choose the Right Way

Sometimes it seems that most people do bad things. Do not copy them.

from Exodus 23:2

It is easy to follow the crowd, but that will only lead to trouble. Choose the way you know is right.

from Matthew 7:13–14

Be Kind

Never be unkind to people who come
from other places and are different from
you.

from Exodus 22:21

Show Respect

Show respect for old people. They are
important, and you must show that in
the way you treat them.

from Leviticus 19:32

Speak Wisely

Good people must be wise in what they say.
They should speak gently to avoid quarrels;
they should be kind and encouraging, not cruel
and insulting; they should never whisper untrue
things about others, but always tell the truth.

from Proverbs 15:1, 4 and 16:27–28

True Riches

Do not spend your life trying to get rich. Even the most wonderful things you can buy just become rubbish in the end. Instead, do what you know is right. Your good deeds will make you rich in heaven – rich forever!

from Matthew 6:19–20

A Happy Home

It is much better to enjoy a simple meal with people you love than to have the most expensive treats with people who are always being nasty to each other.

from Proverbs 15:17

Forgive Others

Jesus told people about forgiveness:

"Sometimes people do wrong things that hurt you. You must forgive them. Then you can be sure that God will forgive you anything you do wrong."

from Matthew 6:14

Love Your Enemies

Jesus said to the people, "Love the people who don't like you; pray for those people who are nasty to you. You are to be good to them just as God is good to them. For God gives the sun and rain to bad people as well as good people."

from Matthew 5:44–45

Love One Another

Jesus said to his friends, "Love one another. You are to love one another in the same way that I have loved you."

from John 13:34

Ten Great Commandments

God spoke all these words, ten great commandments. Here is what God said:

"I am the Lord your God. I rescued you from your enemies. You shall have no other gods but me.

"Do not treat anything else as a god.

"Be careful and respectful when you speak of God.

"God made one day in seven to be a day of rest: keep that day special.

"Respect your father and your mother.

"Do not kill.

"Husbands and wives: you must be completely loyal to one another.

"Do not steal.

"Do not tell lies about others.

"Do not look greedily at the things other people have."

from Exodus 20:1–17, Deuteronomy 5:1–21

Written and compiled by Lois Rock
Illustrations copyright © 2003 by Katherine Lucas
Text copyright © 2003 by Lion Publishing
First published in Great Britain in 2003 by Lion
Publishing.

First U.S. Edition

LCCN: 2003108015

10 9 8 7 6 5 4 3 2 1

Acknowledgments

The extracts in this book have been inspired by or
adapted from the biblical verses noted in each case,
unless otherwise stated. Bible extract on p. 22 quoted
from the Good News Bible, published by The Bible
Societies/HarperCollins Publishers Ltd, UK ©
American Bible Society 1996, 1971, 1976, 1992, used
with permission.

Printed in Singapore

The illustrations for this book were done in acrylic on
textured acrylic paper.

The text was set in Garamond BE.

Little Blessings

FROM THE BIBLE

Lois Rock

Illustrated by Katherine Lucas

 LITTLE, BROWN AND COMPANY

New York ❧ An AOL Time Warner Company

Good Things for You

May God bless you and take care of you.
May God be kind to you and do good
   things for you.
May God look on you with love and give
   you peace.

from Numbers 6:24–26

The World

God bless the towns: may they be peaceful.
God bless the fields: may they be fruitful.
God bless the people: may they be joyful.
May all the world know that God is God.

from Deuteronomy 28:1–14

Harvest

God makes the rich brown earth and sends
  the cool spring rain.

God wakes the tiny seeds and makes the
  seedlings grow.

God gives the world rich harvests: the whole
  world sings for joy!

from Psalm 65

Those Who Do Right

God will bless those who do what is right,
those who say no to wrongdoing.
They will be like trees that grow beside
   a stream,
that stay green in the driest summer
and bear rich fruit at harvest time:
everything they do will go well.

from Psalm 1

Those Who Are Fair

Be fair to others and make this world
   a better place.
God will bless you.

If you see someone being treated unfairly,
   go to help them.
God will bless you.

If you see someone in need, share with
   them what you have.
God will bless you.

God's goodness will shine on you like
   the morning sun.

from Isaiah 58:6–8

Families

May God bless every family. May
the children and the parents and the
grandparents bring each other joy.

from Psalm 115:14

Children

Some people brought their children to Jesus.

He said a blessing prayer: "Let the children come to me and do not stop them. The kingdom of heaven belongs to them."

Jesus placed his hands on them as a sign of blessing, and then they went away.

from Matthew 19:13–15

Those Who Follow Jesus

May God give you all the good
things that will help you to live as
God's friend.

from Hebrews 13:20–21

Those Who Are Worried

God loves you, so don't let anything
worry you or frighten you.

Daniel 10:18

God's Good Things

God will bless poor people:
the kingdom of God belongs to them.

God will bless those who go hungry:
God will fill them with good things.

from Luke 6:20–21

God's Great Reward

God will bless those who weep with sadness:
God will make them laugh with joy.

God will bless those who are bullied and
laughed at as they try to do what is right:
they can be happy inside, knowing that they
will have a great reward in heaven.

from Luke 6:21–23

Evening Blessing

Dear God,
This is my evening prayer:
Teach me to be careful in what I say.
Keep me from wanting to do wrong.
Keep me safe from every danger.

from Psalm 141

Written and compiled by Lois Rock
Illustrations copyright © 2003 by Katherine Lucas
Text copyright © 2003 by Lion Publishing
First published in Great Britain in 2003 by Lion
Publishing.

First U.S. Edition

LCCN: 2003108017

10 9 8 7 6 5 4 3 2 1

Acknowledgments

The extracts in this book have been inspired by or
adapted from the biblical verses noted in each case,
unless otherwise stated.

Printed in Singapore

The illustrations for this book were done in acrylic on
textured acrylic paper.

The text was set in Garamond BE.

Little Psalms

FROM THE BIBLE

Lois Rock

Illustrated by Katherine Lucas

LITTLE, BROWN AND COMPANY

New York ✤ An AOL Time Warner Company

Morning Prayer

Dear God,
Fill us each morning with your love, so
that we may sing and be glad all our life.

from Psalm 90:14

God is Great

God is the king of everything.

The earth is old and its rocks are strong, but
God has been king since before the world.

The ocean is deep and its waves crash and roar,
but God has more power than the mighty sea.

God is God: the One we must obey, the One
we must worship.

from Psalm 93

Praising God

May all the world sing to our God!
The angels in the height,
the sun, the moon, and the silver stars
that glitter in the night;

The oceans and the giant whales,
the storms and wind and rain,
the animals and birds on every
mountain, hill, and plain;

And all the people, young and old,
the wealthy and the poor:
sing praise to God who made the world,
sing praise forevermore!

from Psalm 148

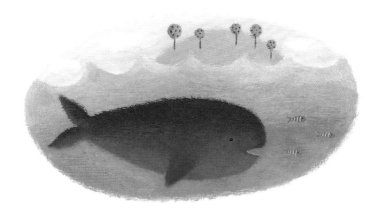

God's Love

Give thanks to God because God is good,
because God's love lasts forever.

from Psalm 118:1

Right and Wrong

Dear God,
Teach me what you mean by right and wrong,
and I will obey.

Doing what is right will make me happy.
It will make me happier than all the money
in the world.

from Psalm 119:33–36

May God Show the Way

Dear God,
Please teach me what you want me to do.
Lead me along a safe path.

from Psalm 27:11

Sorry

Dear God,
I am sorry for what I have done wrong.
Please forgive me.
I am sad about the bad things in me.
Please change me.
I want to be faithful to you, God:
Always love me.

from Psalm 51

When Things Go Wrong

Dear God,
When things go wrong, why do you seem
so far away? Why do you seem to be hiding?

I know you can see what is happening.
I know you help those who need you.

Please listen to my prayer and help me.

from Psalm 10

Trusting God

God is my light and my salvation; I will fear no one.

God protects me from all danger; I will never be afraid.

from Psalm 27:1

God Keep Us Safe

God is our shelter and strength.
God is always ready to help in times
of trouble.

So we will not be afraid, even if the earth is
shaken and mountains fall into the sea.

God is God, and God is greater than all the
things that trouble this world.

With God, we are safe forever.

from Psalm 46

The Good Shepherd

Dear God, you are my shepherd,
You give me all I need:
My food, my drink, a place to rest—
Yes, you are good indeed.

When all the world seems gloomy,
And scary things are near,
You always take good care of me
And so I need not fear.

You've given me such good things
That everyone can see
The very special kindness that
You always show to me.

from Psalm 23

At Nighttime

I lie down to sleep, and I know
that God will keep me safe all
through the night.

from Psalm 4:8

The Prayer Jesus Taught

Our Father, who art in heaven,
hallowed be thy name;
thy kingdom come;
thy will be done;
on earth as it is in heaven.
Give us this day our daily bread.
And forgive us our trespasses,
as we forgive those who trespass against us.
And lead us not into temptation;
but deliver us from evil.
For thine is the kingdom, the power,
and the glory, forever and ever. Amen.

Jesus' prayer
from Matthew 6:9–13, Luke 11:2–4

Dear God, help me to forgive others just as
I want them to forgive me.

Dear God, help me to follow Jesus, and
may I learn to love others as he did.

Praying as Jesus taught
from Matthew 7:12, Matthew 6:14, John 13:34

Loving Others

Dear God, help me to do for others what
I want them to do for me.

Peace on Earth

Dear God,
May the people of the world stop fighting.
May they break up their weapons and
  make something useful instead.

May everyone have a safe place to live.
May everyone enjoy the good things of
  your world.

Praying as Micah encouraged
from Micah 4:3–4

Praying without Words

Dear God,
Help me to pray.
I don't have the right words — only a feeling
deep inside that you can make everything as it
should be.

Praying as Paul taught
from Romans 8:26–27

When Everything Goes Wrong

Dear God,
There are tears in my eyes and tears on my cheeks.
I am all alone and no one can make things better.
Everything has gone wrong. Everything is ruined.

Then I remember you love me forever. You are always
so kind. I can always trust you. As the sun brightens
the morning, you bring me hope.

Prayer of the people of Jerusalem
from Lamentations 1:2 and 3:22–24

When People Are Bad

Dear God,
Sometimes I feel so cross. I want bad things to
happen to bad people.

All the time, I know that you are kind and
loving to everyone. You are just waiting to
forgive them.

I want you to punish them. Why do you have
to be so forgiving?

Jonah's prayer
Jonah 4:2

You made all kinds of animals for every place on earth. There on the hills and the plains, in the green fields and the dry deserts, you take care of them all.

You are a great God. I give you all my respect.

Job's prayer
from Job 38–42

God's Amazing World

Dear God,
I look around and see all the things you
have made: the earth and the sky, the tall
mountains and the deep oceans.

You made the sun that rises every morning and
you scattered huge handfuls of stars in the night-
time sky.

Thanking God

Dear God,
Thank you for being so good to us.
Thank you for listening to our prayers.
Thank you for the world we live in:
the summer and the winter,
the sunshine and the rain;
the time for sowing seeds
and the time to gather crops.
Thank you for all the good things
   the world gives to us.

A psalm of David
from Psalm 65

Away from Home

Dear God,
Show me that you are my God.
Take care of me on my journey.
Make sure that I have food and everything
  I need.
Most of all, bring me safely home.

Jacob's prayer
from Genesis 28:20–21

Right and Wrong

Dear God,
Please make me wise: help me to know
what is right and what is wrong.

Solomon's prayer
from 1 Kings 3:9

Listening to God

Speak to me, dear God.
I want to live my life for you,
and I am listening to what you
have to say to me.

Samuel's prayer
from 1 Samuel 3:10

Coming to Pray

Dear God,
Here I am, all alone, in this quiet place.
I have come to pray to you.

Praying as Jesus taught
from Matthew 6:6

Little Prayers

FROM THE BIBLE

Lois Rock

Illustrated by Katherine Lucas

LITTLE, BROWN AND COMPANY

New York ❧ An AOL Time Warner Company

Written and compiled by Lois Rock
Illustrations copyright © 2003 by Katherine Lucas
Text copyright © 2003 by Lion Publishing
First published in Great Britain in 2003 by Lion
Publishing.

First U.S. Edition
LCCN: 2003108016

10 9 8 7 6 5 4 3 2 1

Acknowledgments
The extracts in this book have been inspired by or
adapted from the biblical verses noted in each case,
unless otherwise stated. Material from *The Alternative
Service Book*, 1980 (p. 28) is copyright © The
Archbishop's Council. Extract reproduced by
permission.

Printed in Singapore

The illustrations for this book were done in acrylic on
textured acrylic paper.

The text was set in Garamond BE.